Come, See the Wonder

Four complete Christmas programs for schools and churches

Gail Gaymer Martin

STANDARD
PUBLISHING
Cincinnati, Ohio

Dedication

With much love to Kelly Maher, Amanda, Alex and Ian Pineau, Camille Stanfield, and granddaughter, Nicole. May the joy and blessings of Christmas be with you always.

Permission is granted to reproduce these programs for ministry purposes only—not for resale.

The Standard Publishing Company, Cincinnati, Ohio
A division of Standex International Corporation

© 1997 by Gail Gaymer Martin
All rights reserved
Printed in the United States of America

04 03 02 01 00 99 98 97   5 4 3 2 1

ISBN 0-7847-0701-4

Table of Contents

Introduction

The four Christmas services in this book are appropriate for Sunday school programs or Christian school programs. They are designed for easy production with no special lighting or settings necessary. They may be presented in the church sanctuary or on a stage. There are a few props needed and minimal costuming. The plays are written so that very little memorization is needed. They are designed to be read either from the script placed on a stand or on note cards carried by the children. The parts are simple enough, in most cases, that younger children who cannot read may memorize a simple line or two. The program is written to involve children of all ages. The action moves from scene to scene with an occasional interlude in the form of a suggested carol which is either sung by the children or by the entire congregation or audience. The Bible verses are from the Holy Bible, New International Version.

Three of the four programs are accompanied by an Advent activity. Advent is a preparation for the season of Christmas and the activities are used as part of the Christmas program. The program which does not include an Advent activity is *Christmas Letters*.

Each program includes congregational carols as well as responsory material and prayers. This part of the program may be lead by a minister or another adult leader.

The book is arranged in the following format: an introduction to the program, the Advent activity, the printed bulletin/program format, and the script.

Christmas Prayers

Introduction

This children's Christmas service focuses on prayer, teaching the children to acknowledge the needs of all people, not just their own needs. It also identifies that prayer includes praise and thanksgiving, as well as intercessions. Using the Christmas story as a catalyst for prayer requests, the children talk about prayer and the story of Jesus' birth and God's plan for our salvation.

The script is written so that it may be read. Children should rehearse enough so that the reading flows, as if speaking. The dialogue has fifteen speaking parts and the prayer is divided into seven parts. The prayer may also be divided into shorter readings to include more children. It may be written on cards to accommodate reading rather than memorization.

The children come forward in sets of three, standing behind decorated music stands or podiums adapted to the children's height. These stands should be located center stage. It is possible, with risers, to use a pulpit and lectern and only one stand in the center of the chancel. No costumes are necessary for this program.

During *The Prayer* portion of the script, the children come forward in groups so that they all gather at the front for the final "Amen" and recessional. Each prayer section will be read by one child from each group or it may be divided by sentences giving more than one child the opportunity to participate in the prayer. Each group will carry a Prayer Banner which is described more fully under *Advent Activities*. As each group of children complete their portion of the prayer, they will move back allowing the next group to come forward. The children displaying the banner for each prayer section will stand front and center, and, then, move back to allow the next banner to be displayed.

All musical selections are optional, except the carol response, "Angels We Have Heard on High," which is sung by everyone.

Advent activities are suggested as a way to prepare the children for Christmas and the Christmas service. The Advent activities follow this introduction. Then a guide for a printed bulletin or program format is presented, followed by the Christmas program *Script*.

Advent Activities

Advent is a time of preparation and anticipation of Christmas. During Advent, it is appropriate that children also begin to prepare for Christmas. This children's program offers two Advent activities in preparation for Christmas.

First, it is good that children learn a lesson in generosity; "It is more blessed to give than to receive" (Acts 20:35). Since Christmas is a time of generosity and giving, it is suggested that the children participate in a project which involves giving to the needy. This project may be in cooperation with a church or school project or may be independent. A hat and mitten collection, a canned/dried food collection, Christmas food baskets, or toy collection, for example, could be gathered and designated to some umbrella organization or special mission project of your church or school.

Second, prayer banners which will be used during the Christmas program may be made as an Advent activity. These banners can be made freehand on poster board, colored and decorated, or they could be made from felt or some other material and decorated by the children. Each banner highlights a key word from sections of the prayer. These words are: Our Leaders, Goodwill, Work, Peace, Family, and Jesus. For example, Goodwill may be decorated with pictures of canned goods, money, mittens, handshakes, etc. Other banners may be designed as desired.

Bulletin/Program Format

Welcome
Congregation: "Hark! the Herald Angels Sing"
(Children enter during the congregational carol.)
Opening: *(All rise.)*
Leader: The angel said to them, . . . "This will be a sign to
you: You will find a baby wrapped in cloths and lying in
a manger."
Carol response: "Angels We Have Heard on High" *(vs. 1)*
**All sing: Angels we have heard on high, Sweetly singing
o'er the plains, And the mountains in reply, Echoing
their joyous strains. *(Refrain:)* Gloria in excelsis Deo,
Gloria in excelsis Deo.**
Leader: The shepherds said to one another, "Let's go to
Bethlehem and see this thing that has happened, which
the Lord has told us about."
Carol response: "Angels We Have Heard on High" *(vs. 2)*
**All sing: Shepherds, why this jubilee? Why your joyous
strains prolong? What the gladsome tidings be,
Which inspire your heav'nly song? *(Refrain)* Gloria in
excelsis Deo, Gloria in excelsis Deo.**
Leader: So they hurried off and found Mary and Joseph,
and the baby who was lying in the manger.
Carol response: "Angels We Have Heard on High" *(vs. 3)*
**All sing: Come to Bethlehem, and see, Him whose birth
the angels sing; Come, adore on bended knee, Christ
the Lord, our newborn King. *(Refrain)* Gloria in excelsis
Deo, Gloria in excelsis Deo.**
(Please be seated.)
(Reading from Luke 11:9, 10, Mark 11:24.)
Leader: Jesus was asked about prayer and he said, "Ask
and it will be given to you; seek and you will find;
knock and the door will be opened to you. For everyone
who asks receives; he who seeks finds; and to him who
knocks, the door will be opened." Jesus said, "Whatever
you ask for in prayer, believe that you have received it,

and it will be yours." And now, the children will present *Christmas Prayers.*

Children's Carol: "Oh Come, Little Children"

Christmas Prayers

Introduction - *(Children's names may be listed.)*

First Reading: Luke 2:1-5 *(Children's names may be listed.)*

Second Reading: Luke 2:6, 7 *(Children's names may be listed.)*

Little Children's Carol: "Away in a Manger"

Third Reading: Luke 2:8-14 *(Children's names may be listed.)*

Fourth Reading: Luke 2:15-20 *(Children's names may be listed.)*

Children's Carol: "Silent Night! Holy Night!"

The Children's Prayer: *(Readers' names may be listed.)*

All: The Lord's Prayer
Congregation: "Joy to the World!"
      (Children recess during congregational carol.)

Script

(Three music stands or podiums low enough to accommodate the children's height are decorated with Christmas garland and ribbon and placed center stage. Children will read their lines from these stands. They read, as if speaking. Three children stand behind the stands. Child 2, in the middle, has his or her eyes closed and fingers crossed.)

INTRODUCTION

Child 1: What are you doing? You have your eyes closed and your fingers crossed?

Child 2: I was thinking about what gifts I want for Christmas. I was wishing for a couple of new computer games.

Child 1: No sense *wishing!* When I want something, I *pray* for it. I ask God to bring me a dirt bike, and, I know God answers prayers, so—the bike is mine!

Child 3: Excuse me, but I think you have a misunderstanding about prayer. I'm not sure that computer games or a new dirt bike fits that description. God doesn't promise to answer prayers that are asking for unnecessary, foolish or hurtful things. *Prayer* is talking to God, and in it, we do much more than ask for things. In prayer, we give *thanks* for what we have received, we *praise* God for his goodness and mercy and, then, we ask God for our *daily* needs.

Child 1: It's Christmas. Maybe, we should be asking for special gifts at Christmas, not just for ourselves, but for *others.*

Child 2: Yes, Christmas is a time of "Peace on earth and goodwill to all people." Our prayers should include the needs of the world. Maybe, we can get some ideas as we read the Christmas story from the Bible.

Child 3: That's a good idea. Let's get started.

(Three children exit, as three new children go behind the stands. Child 4 carries a Bible and uses the center stand. All children reading from the Bible will use the center stand.)

Christmas Prayers

FIRST READING

Child 4 (*reads from Luke 2:1-5*)**:** In those days Caesar Augustus issued a decree that a census should be taken of the entire Roman world. (This was the first census that took place while Quirinius was governor of Syria.) And everyone went to his own town to register. So Joseph also went up from the town of Nazareth in Galilee to Judea, to Bethlehem the town of David, because he belonged to the house and line of David. He went there to register with Mary, who was pledged to be married to him and was expecting a child.

Child 5: What do you think? This reading seems to be about laws and taxes.

Child 6: Yes, but it's really about government. We should always pray for our government—for our president and governor, and all our leaders.

Child 4: There are other leaders too—leaders in our church and school.

Child 5: And don't forget our Sunday school teachers. Let's get started.

(They exit as three more children come forward. Child 7 will read from the center stand.)

SECOND READING

Child 7 (*reads from Luke 2:6, 7*)**:** While they were there, the time came for the baby to be born, and she gave birth to her firstborn, a son. She wrapped him in cloths and placed him in a manger, because there was no room for them in the inn.

Child 8: I think that what the innkeeper did was important. He was kind and helpful. He gave Joseph and Mary a place to rest and a place where Jesus could be born.

Child 9: People are generous, especially, at Christmas, like our Sunday school (*or church*) project; people have donated (*be specific and name the food, mitten, Christmas gift project, etc. in which you have been currently involved*) to help people in need.

Child 8: What about praying for people who are homeless, like Joseph and Mary would have been if the innkeeper hadn't helped them?

Child 7: We have many things to include in our Christmas prayer.

(The three exit. The younger children will come forward to sing, "Away in a Manger.")

LITTLE CHILDREN'S CAROL: "Away in a Manger"
(As the carol ends, the younger children are seated and three new children come forward. Child 10 reads from the center stand.)

THIRD READING

Child 10 *(reads from Luke 2:8-14):* And there were shepherds living out in the fields nearby, keeping watch over their flocks at night. An angel of the Lord appeared to them, and the glory of the Lord shone around them, and they were terrified. But the angel said to them, "Do not be afraid. I bring you good news of great joy that will be for all the people. Today in the town of David a Savior has been born to you; he is Christ the Lord. This will be a sign to you: You will find a baby wrapped in cloths and lying in a manger." Suddenly a great company of the heavenly host appeared with the angel, praising God and saying, "Glory to God in the highest, and on earth peace to men on whom his favor rests."

Child 11: I think the message of the angels is important. It tells us that because Jesus was born we can be at peace, knowing that we are with Him on earth and that we will be with Him in Heaven.

Child 10: They also mentioned *goodwill.* We should be kind to people and try to get along.

Child 12: What about the shepherds? They were doing their work, watching the sheep, and God sent the message to them first, not to kings or rulers.

Child 11: Oh, yes, God loves all people, rich and poor. As you said, the shepherds were at their job; we should be thankful for jobs—no matter how important or simple they are. Not all people have jobs that enable them to support their families.

Child 12: We also have much to pray for. Let's get busy.
(They exit. The next three children come forward. Child 13 reads from the center stand.)

FOURTH READING

Child 13 *(reads from Luke 2:15-20):* When the angels had left them and gone into heaven, the shepherds said to one another, "Let's go to Bethlehem and see this thing that has happened, which the Lord has told us about." So they hurried off and found Mary and Joseph, and the baby, who was lying in the manger. When they had seen him, they spread the word concerning what had been told them about this child, and all who heard it were amazed at what the shepherds said to them. But Mary treasured up all these things and pondered them in her heart. The shepherds returned, glorifying and praising God for all the things they had heard and seen, which were just as they had been told.

Child 14: What I like about this Bible reading is that God *guided* the shepherds to the stable. The angels said "Here's a sign for you—the baby will be in a manger"— and sure enough there He was.

Child 13: In the stable, the shepherds found a mother, father, and child—a family. We should be thankful for *families,* for mothers and fathers who love us and care for us.

Child 15: I like how *excited* the shepherds were. I can imagine them running through the town telling all the people the wonderful story of Jesus' birth.

Child 14: We are supposed to tell others about Jesus, everywhere we go. Let's add that to our prayer.
(They exit. The children who will sing "Silent Night! Holy Night!" come forward.)

CHILDREN'S CAROL: "Silent Night! Holy Night!"

(Stands are removed during the hymn. Children come forward in small groups. Each group is holding the banner which is appropriate for the various sections of the prayer. Each child should be ready to speak as the previous child finishes; the prayer should flow without a break. As each group finishes their portion of the prayer, they will step back allowing the next group to come forward. The banner for each section should be displayed, front and center, and, then, they too move back to accommodate the next banner.)

THE CHILDREN'S PRAYER:

Prayer 1: Heavenly Father on this special night, we come to You with our Christmas prayers, not for material things or things only for ourselves, but for the needs of all people.

Prayer 2: *(Banner:* OUR LEADERS) This Christmas, we ask You to bless all of our leaders—our president and governor, and all public officials. We also ask You to bless our church leaders and Sunday school teachers. We pray for our school teachers and principals and we ask You to bless the work that they do.

Prayer 3: *(Banner:* GOODWILL) Heavenly Father, at Christmas and all the year through, bless the homeless and hungry. Give them hope, and help all of us to see their need and share with them the plenty that You have given us.

Prayer 4: *(Banner:* WORK) Father, we ask You to bless all the employers and workers. Help people to be fair and honest in their work. We ask You to give courage to those who do not have work. Help them to find jobs, so they may support their families and have hope for the future.

Prayer 5: *(Banner:* PEACE) God, our Father, we ask for peace in the world, that countries stop fighting and learn to work together. We ask that people will learn to not treat others badly, because of the color of their skin, their religion or nationality. We thank You for the peace You give us because of our salvation through Jesus' birth.

Prayer 6: *(Banner:* FAMILY) Father, we thank You for loving families—for moms and dads, brothers and sisters, and grandparents. We thank You for all the people important in our lives, including our church family.

Prayer 7: *(Banner:* JESUS) And finally Lord, we thank You for the best Christmas gift of all, Your Son, Jesus who gives us eternal life. We ask You to continue to guide us and help us to tell others about You and the salvation we have in Jesus. We pray in His name.

All Children: Amen.

All: The Lord's Prayer
(As the children recess down the aisle, they display the banners.)

CONGREGATION: "Joy to the World!"

A Capital C.H.R.I.S.T.M.A.S.

Introduction

A Capital C.H.R.I.S.T.M.A.S. is a Christmas service for children in either a Sunday school or Christian school setting. This program tells the Christmas story highlighted by a letter of the alphabet from a key word in the telling of the Christmas story. Eventually when these alphabet letters are rearranged, they spell the word CHRISTMAS. This is done as the children present a Christmas poem.

The script has been written so that a few or many children may participate. Each speaking part has been subdivided with each sentence numbered so that different children can be assigned one or more of the lines. Having fewer lines makes memorization easier for the children. If the parts are to be read, the children may carry them on a note card, or, if only one child is to do the part, the sentences may be placed on the back of the poster which the child carries and may be easily read in that way. The Group line may be delivered *before* as well as after the speaker, if so desired. The Christmas Poem may be read by *one* child while other children display the Capital Letter posters.

The capital letters are posters and made as an Advent activity which is described more fully in the next section.

Music selections are suggested. They may be altered to fit the needs or desires of the presenters. The music may be done by small groups or classes, a junior choir, or individual soloists. Student instrumentalists may also be used to enhance the program and involve more children.

The program is outlined in a printed bulletin or program format with space for listing specific music and the names of the children or classes participating. The Leader may be a Sunday school leader or teacher, or it may be a minister. The *Advent Activity* and the *Script* are printed separately.

Advent Activity

Advent is a time of preparation and anticipation of Christmas. This Advent activity will begin to prepare the children for the Christmas season.

Capital letters spelling Christmas are used as part of the Christmas program. Nine groups or classes will decorate large capital letters made from poster board which spell out the word, **CHRISTMAS.** Each letter can be decorated in various colors, designs, and using a variety of media, such as sparkle paint, collage, attached items (such as straw), children's drawings, or whatever the imagination of the children envisions.

The letters needed, their meaning, and some possible suggestions for drawings follow:

R Root of Jesse—tree stump, tree branch, star.
C Caesar Augustus—scrolled document, Bethlehem, Roman figures.
T Traveler—travelers with donkey.
I Innkeeper—stable, animals, straw, inn, manger.
S Shepherds—shepherds, shepherd crook, sheep, star.
A Angels—angels, star, words: Gloria, etc.
M Manger—manger, Joseph, Mary and Jesus, stable, animals, straw.
S Savior—baby Jesus, manger, cross.
H Holy night—silhouetted city of Bethlehem, stars, nativity.

Bulletin/Program Format

Welcome
Congregation: "O Come, Little Children"
Opening: *(All rise.)*
Leader: For to us a child is born, to us a son is given, and the
    government will be on his shoulders. And he will be called
    Wonderful Counselor, Mighty God, Everlasting Father,
    Prince of Peace. Arise, shine, for your light has come,
All: And the glory of the Lord has risen upon us.
Leader: Praise the Lord! Praise Him in His sanctuary.
All: Praise Him in the heavens.
Leader: Praise Him for His mighty deeds; Praise Him for His
    exceeding greatness!
All: Let everything that breathes, praise the Lord! Glory to
    God in the highest.
Leader: Let us pray. Lord You told us to come to You like a lit-
    tle child. In that innocence, we give thanks for the child
    born to us in Bethlehem so many years ago. Help us always
    to approach the Christmas season with the joy and wonder
    of a child. In the name of the holy Babe, we pray.
All: Amen.
(Please be seated.)

The Presentation: Selected verses from Isaiah and Luke 2:1-
    20 as told by the children.

The Letter: *R—The Root of Jesse*
(Children or class who participates will be listed here.)
The Letter: *C—Caesar Augustus*
(Children or class who participates will be listed here.)

Congregation: "O Little Town of Bethlehem"

The Letter: *T—Travelers*
(Children or class who participates will be listed here.)
The Letter: *I—Innkeeper*

A Capital C.H.R.I.S.T.M.A.S.

(Children or class who participates will be listed here.)

Children's Anthem: "Why Was He Born in a Stable?" *(M. Posegate)*

The Letter: *S —Shepherds*
(Children or class who participates will be listed here.)
The Letter: *A—Angels*
(Children or class who participates will be listed here.)

Congregation: "Hark! the Herald Angels Sing"

The Letter: *M—Manger*
(Children or class who participates will be listed here.)

Children's Carol: "Away in a Manger"

The Letter: *S—Savior*
(Children or class who participates will be listed here.)
The Letter: *H—Holy night*
(Children or class who participates will be listed here.)

Children's Carol: "Silent Night! Holy Night!"

The Christmas Poem
> C —The **Christ child** in the manger lay,
> H —In swaddling clothes upon the **hay.**
> R —There, our **Redeemer** came to earth,
> I —An **infant** born of lowly birth.
> S —The **shepherds** heard the angels sing,
> T —And **traveled** to the newborn King,
> M —Where **Mary** and Joseph joined their praise.
> A —Now, we our **Alleluias** raise.
> S —A **Savior** given from Heaven above,
> All —God's Christmas gift of endless love.

Recessional Hymn: "Joy to the World!"

A Capital C.H.R.I.S.T.M.A.S.

Script

(The first group rises; one child holds a large decorated R. The lines may be spoken by one or more children by assigning numbered sentences. The group line may be delivered before or after the speaker or at both times.)

The Letter: R
Group: R stands for the "Root of Jesse."
Speaker(s): (1) In the Old Testament, prophets foretold the birth of Jesus. (2) The prophet Isaiah wrote that out of the root of Jesse a branch would grow. (3) This branch would rule the Gentiles and bring light to a darkened world.
(They are seated. The second group rises; one child holds the letter C.)

The Letter: C
Group: C stands for Caesar Augustus.
Speaker(s): (1) In the Gospel of Luke, we are told there was a decree from Caesar Augustus that all people had to register for a tax. (2) Each family was to register in the city of its family's origin. (3) Joseph had to go to the city of David which was Bethlehem. (4) This was also in the prophecies that the Messiah would be born in Bethlehem.
(The children are seated.)

CONGREGATION: "O Little Town of Bethlehem"
(The third group rises; one child holds the letter T.)

The Letter: T
Group: T stands for Travelers.
Speaker(s): (1) People from near and far traveled toward Bethlehem. (2) The roads were crowded with people walking or riding donkeys. (3) Among them were Joseph and Mary. (4) Mary's baby was to be born very soon and the trip was long and tiring.

A Capital C.H.R.I.S.T.M.A.S.

(The children are seated. The fourth group rises; one child holds the letter I.)

The Letter: I
Group: **I** stands for Innkeeper.
Speaker(s): (1) When Mary and Joseph arrived in Bethlehem, it was very crowded and they could not find a place to stay. (2) An innkeeper, who had no room left in his inn, told Joseph that they could rest in the stable. (3) It was there in that humble place that Jesus was born. (4) Only the animals were there to see this wonderful miracle.
(The previous group of children rises and joins the song. If it is a congregation hymn, they will be seated.)

CHILDREN'S ANTHEM: "Why Was He Born in a Stable?" *(M. Posegate)*

(The children are seated. The fifth group rises; one child holds the letter S.)

The Letter: S
Group: **S** stands for Shepherds.
Speaker(s): (1) On the hills outside Bethlehem shepherds were watching their flocks of sheep. (2) The shepherds spent many evenings outside and they were familiar with the night sky. (3) On this night, the shepherds knew that something unusual was happening; they saw a brightness in the sky over Bethlehem which they had never seen before.
(The children are seated. Group six rises; one child holds an A.)

The Letter: A
Group: **A** stands for Angels.
Speaker(s): (1)As the shepherds were looking into the sky, an angel appeared and told them that a Savior had been born in Bethlehem; they would find him lying in a

A Capital C.H.R.I.S.T.M.A.S.

manger. (2) Suddenly, the sky was filled with angels praising God.
(All are seated.)

CONGREGATION: "Hark! the Herald Angels Sing"
(The children are seated. The seventh group rises; one child holds an M.)

The Letter: M
Group: M stands for Manger.
Speaker(s): (1) The shepherds hurried to Bethlehem and found the stable. (2) There, they found Mary and Joseph and, in the manger, lay the newborn baby, Jesus wrapped in pieces of cloth.

(They may be joined by the preschool class to sing.)

CHILDREN'S CAROL: "Away in a Manger"
(The children are seated. The eighth group rises; one child holds the letter S.)

The Letter: S
Group: S stands for Savior.
Speaker(s): (1) The shepherds told Mary and Joseph all that had happened to them on the hillside outside Bethlehem. (2) They told, in wonder, how the heavenly angels praised God. (3) Joseph remembered the angel who had appeared to him and told him that Mary would give birth to God's Son, the Savior of the world.
(The children are seated. The final group rises; one child holds the letter H.)

The Letter: H
Group: H is for Holy Night.
Speaker(s): (1) And so it was, so many years ago, that God touched the earth in the form of a tiny child, born of a virgin in a lowly stable on that holy night. (2) This little

A Capital C.H.R.I.S.T.M.A.S.

baby, as the prophets said, was to become the King of kings, the Savior of the world.
(*They are all seated.*)

CHILDREN'S CAROL: "Silent Night! Holy Night!"

(*Following the song, one child rises with the letter C, either reciting or having someone else read a line from the Christmas poem. Each child in order presents his letter to spell Christmas. The last line is said by all of the children. When the poem is completed, the letters spelling "CHRISTMAS" will be across the front of the church.*)

      C —The **Christ child** in the manger lay,
      H —In swaddling clothes upon the **hay.**
      R —There, our **Redeemer** came to earth,
       I —An **infant** born of lowly birth.
      S —The **shepherds** heard the angels sing,
      T —And **traveled** to the newborn King,
     M —Where **Mary** and Joseph joined their praise.
     A —Now, we our **Alleluias** raise.
     S —A **Savior** given from Heaven above,
   All —God's Christmas gift of endless love.

(*As the children and teachers recess down the aisle, the letters of Christmas, in order, will lead the recession.*)

RECESSIONAL HYMN: "Joy to the World!"

Christmas Letters

Introduction

Christmas Letters is a children's Christmas service suitable for Sunday school or a Christian school. The program is written for twelve specific characters as well as shepherds and angels which may be one or more children. It has been written with minimal memorization. Only three characters, the mother, boy and girl must memorize a small number of lines. All other parts, which include: six modern day children, Joseph, Mary, and the Innkeeper, are written as letters, so that they may be read. A microphone may be used, if needed.

Other children will be involved in singing the songs interspersed throughout the program. Also, children with musical abilities may provide additional instrumental music during the program.

The letters written from the shepherd and the angel may be divided into shorter responses, so that the part may be assigned to more children. The letter preceding those readings would then be addressed to "Dear Shepherds" or "Dear Angels", rather than the singular.

The letters written to the biblical characters will be signed by the name of the actual child reading the letter, and the biblical character will address the answer to that specific child's name. If the letters are assigned in smaller parts to involve more children, the Bible character may answer, "Dear Children" or "Dear _____ and _____ " for example.

For greater effect, the modern letters will be written on plain writing or typing paper, but the letters of the biblical characters should be on a parchment-type paper or buff colored paper and should be rolled like a scroll.

Simple costuming should be used for the various

biblical characters. The modern day children will dress as they are. The mother could wear an apron or dress in a more mature style. Another option would be to use an older student or an adult, such as a Sunday school teacher for that role.

The song words written for this program are sung to the tune of the traditional Christmas carol, *"Venite Adoremus."* The verses are to be sung one at a time by groups of children as appropriate after each set of readings, as is indicated in the *Script*. The refrain may be sung by all of the children and may also include the congregation or audience. The groups of children who sing each verse may be divided by Sunday school class, grade level, or some other method. An arrangement of the "Christmas Letters" song is included, and the words are printed in their entirety on one page, also, for easy distribution for memorizing.

The program is outlined in a printed bulletin or program format. Specific music selections, the names of children or classes participating, and other information should be added to meet the individual needs of the church or school presenting the program. The *Script* is printed separately.

Bulletin/Program Format

Welcome
Congregation: "Joy to the World!"
Opening: *(All rise.)*
Leader: He said to them, "Let the little children come to me, and do not hinder them, for the kingdom of God belongs to such as these. I tell you the truth, anyone who will not receive the kingdom of God like a little child will never enter it" (Mark 10:14, 15).
All: Glory to God in the highest and on earth peace among those whom He favors.
Leader: Let us pray. Lord You blessed the little children. As You have told us, we are all Your children. You care for us, guide us, forgive us, and You gave us Your Son, the Babe of Bethlehem, as our Savior. We thank You and praise You in the name of Him whose birth we celebrate.
All: Amen.
(Please be seated.)
Congregation: "Oh Come, Little Children"

Presentation of the Christmas Letters
Mother, Boy and Girl -

Letter to Joseph
Child 1 -
Joseph -
Song of Joseph -
All *(Refrain):* **Oh Jesus, Holy Babe, from Heaven above, You came to earth to be God's saving love.**

Letter to Mary
Child 2 -
Mary -
Song of Mary -
All *(Refrain):* **Oh Jesus, Holy Babe, from Heaven above, You came to earth to be God's saving love.**

Letter to the Innkeeper

Child 3 -

Innkeeper -

Song of the Innkeeper -

All *(Refrain):* **Oh Jesus, Holy Babe, from Heaven above, You came to earth to be God's saving love.**

Congregation: "O Little Town of Bethlehem"

Letter to the Shepherd

Child 4 -

Shepherd(s) -

Song of the Shepherds -

All *(Refrain):* **Oh Jesus, Holy Babe, from Heaven above, You came to earth to be God's saving love.**

Letter to the Angel

Child 5 -

Angel(s) -

Song of the Angels -

All *(Refrain):* **Oh Jesus, Holy Babe, from Heaven above, You came to earth to be God's saving love.**

Letter to the baby Jesus

Child 6 -

Children's Song: "Away in a Manger"

Leader: Ah, dearest Jesus, holy child, make Thee a bed soft undefiled within my heart that it may be a quiet chamber kept for Thee.

All: Amen.

Congregation: "Hark! the Herald Angels Sing"

Christmas Letters

Christmas Letters

Venite Adoremus

Gail Gaymer Martin

traditional melody

To | Jo - | seph | long | a - | go, | an | an - | gel | came
Oh, | Mar - | y, | vir - | gin | pure, | the | cho - | sen | one
Then | on | that | ho - | ly | night | in | Beth - | le - | hem
The | shep - | herds | watched | the | sky | o'er | Beth - | le - | hem;
With | an - | gels' | joy - | ful | news, | may | hearts | be | stirred,

And | told | him | do | not | fear, | and | | feel | no | shame.
To | be | the | moth - | er | of | God's | | on - | ly | Son.
No | room | was | there | to | house | our | | God - | made | man.
They | saw | a | star | a - | glow, | and | | won - | dered | then.
The | plan | for | our | sal - | va - | tion, | | God's | own | Word.

For | Mar - | y | was | to | be | a | | moth - | er | mild,
To | Beth - | le - | hem | You | came | by | | law's | de - | cree,
An | inn - | keep - | er, | in | kind - | ness, | | saw | their | plight,
The | heav - | ens | soon | were | filled | with | | an - | gels | bright
Then | sing | we | now | the | an - | gels' | | song | a - | gain,

To | bear | on | earth | God's | Son, | a | | Ho - | ly | Child.
God's | plan | for | us, | so | told | in | | pro - | phe - | cy.
A | man - | ger | was | Christ's | bed | that | | bles - | sed | night.
Who | told | them | of | the | Sav - | ior | | born | that | night.
"Glo - | ry | to | God | on | high | and | | peace | to | men."

Arr. by Gail Gaymer Martin

Oh, Je - sus, Ho - ly Babe, from heav'n a - bove,

You came to earth to be God's sav - ing love.

Christmas Letters

(Sung to the Traditional Carol: *Venite Adoremus*, Words: *Gail Gaymer Martin*)

To Joseph long ago, an angel came
And told him do not fear, and feel no shame.
For Mary was to be a mother mild,
To bear on earth God's Son, a Holy Child.
Refrain:
Oh Jesus, Holy Babe, from Heaven above,
You came to earth to be God's saving love.

Oh, Mary, virgin pure, the chosen one
To be the mother of God's only Son.
To Bethlehem, you came by law's decree,
God's plan for us, so told in prophecy.
Refrain:

Then on that holy night in Bethlehem
No room was there to house, our God made-man.
An innkeeper, in kindness, saw their plight,
A manger was Christ's bed that blessed night.
Refrain:

The shepherds watched the sky o'er Bethlehem;
They saw a star aglow, and wondered then.
The heavens soon were filled with angels bright
Who told them of the Savior born that night.
Refrain:

With angels' joyful news, may hearts be stirred,
The plan for our salvation, God's own Word.
Then, sing we now the angels' song again,
"Glory to God on high, and peace to men."
Refrain:

Christmas Letters

Script

(Mother enters with a letter in her hand.)

Mother: Here's a letter to you from Grandma. *(She sits on a chair.)* Come here and listen. *(Children sit at her feet.)*
Dear Grandchildren,

Because your Grandpa is recovering from a bad case of the flu, we cannot be with you this Christmas, but you are always in our minds and hearts even when miles separate us.

Our Christmas gifts to you will arrive in the mail, but the best gift I can give you cannot be delivered by the post office. It is our gift of love to you, just as Christmas celebrates the best gift of all, God's love to us through the birth of Jesus.

As you enjoy all the Christmas surprises, always keep God's gift centered in your heart for that is the *most* important and precious gift you will receive.

All our love,

Grandma and Grandpa

It's nice Grandma let you know why she can't come and also what Christmas means to her. Letters are wonderful ways to share our news and our thoughts.

Girl *(rising):* Let's write a letter to Grandma after Christmas and tell her all of the things that happened here during the holiday. *(Boy rises.)*

Boy: Good idea. You know, *(Pause.)* what if we could write letters and find out about all the things that happened when Jesus was born?

Girl: The *Bible* tells us what happened!

Boy: But I mean like how the shepherds *felt* when the angels sang "Glory to God in the Highest."

Girl: That would be interesting! We could write to Joseph and Mary and even the baby Jesus. Just imagine—

(As the first reader steps forward, the other characters are seated.)

Letter to Joseph

Child 1: *(The first child steps forward with a letter and reads.)*
Dear Joseph,

The Bible tells us that an angel appeared to you in a dream and told you about Mary and the Baby Jesus. Were you frightened when you saw the angel? How did you feel when you were told that Mary was going to have a baby? Did you wish you didn't have to go to Bethlehem?

Love, (Child 1)

(Child 1 exits, as Joseph enters.)

Joseph: *(An older child dressed as Joseph walks forward; opens the scroll and reads.)*
Dear *(Child 1)*,

After I was engaged to Mary, I learned that she was expecting a baby. I was upset and very surprised. I could not believe this news. I did not want to hurt Mary or embarrass her, but I thought that perhaps I should not marry her? I didn't know the right thing to do; I was very confused. I thought I would just quietly tell her that we would *not* be married.

One night an angel came to me in a dream, and when I woke I thought about what the angel had said. I wasn't really frightened of the angel, because it was like a dream, but I was astounded. I knew that it was a message from God. The angel told me that I should make Mary my wife without being fearful. He explained the baby was from the Holy Spirit. I did what the angel told me and took Mary as my wife and cared for her and for Jesus when He was born.

I was worried about the trip to Bethlehem, which was necessary to make, because I knew it was a long journey. It was prophesied in the Bible that Jesus was to be born there. The prophecy said, "But you, Bethlehem, in the land of Judah, are by no means least among the rulers of Judah; for out of you will come a ruler who will be the shepherd of my people Israel"(Matthew 2:6). I knew that this journey happened according to God's plan.

Signed, Joseph

(Joseph exits. Children come forward for the song, sung to the tune "Venite Adoremus.")

Christmas Letters

Song of Joseph: To Joseph long ago, an angel came.
　　　　And told him do not fear, and feel no shame.
　　　　For Mary was to be a mother mild,
　　　　To bear on earth God's Son, a Holy Child.
All *(Refrain):* **Oh Jesus, Holy Babe, from Heaven above,**
　You came to earth to be God's saving love.

Letter to Mary
Child 2: *(Child 2 walks forward and reads.)*
Dear Mary,

How exciting to be the mother of Jesus! How did you feel when *you* were told by the angel that you were to have God's son? Were you worried about what people would say? Were you afraid to travel to Bethlehem, so close to Jesus' birth, to register for the tax?

Love, *(Child 2)*

(As Child 2 exits, Mary rises.)
Mary: *(An older child steps forward dressed as Mary and reads.)*
Dear *(Child 2),*

When the angel appeared to me, I was frightened, but he quickly told me not to be afraid. When I learned that I was to be the mother of God's son, I could not believe it. I was unmarried. I was not a special person. I didn't understand why I was chosen. I didn't even have time to think about what people would say or what *Joseph* would say. All I knew was that I was chosen by God and I felt very blessed. I praised Him and I thanked Him for the opportunity to serve Him.

It was very difficult to travel to Bethlehem. The trip was long and took days to get there. Joseph tried to make the trip easier by placing me on the donkey, but I was very uncomfortable, because the baby was to be born very soon. We were so discouraged when we got to Bethlehem and could not find a place to stay. A kind innkeeper let us use his stable and that is where Jesus was born.

Signed, Mary

Christmas Letters

(Mary exits. Children come forward for the song, sung to the tune "Venite Adoremus.")

Song of Mary: Oh, Mary, virgin pure, the chosen one
To be the mother of God's only Son.
To Bethlehem, you came by law's decree
God's plan for us, so told in prophecy.

All *(Refrain):* **Oh Jesus, Holy Babe, from Heaven above,
You came to earth to be God's saving love.**

Letter to the Innkeeper

Child 3: *(Child 3 comes forward with a letter and reads.)*
Dear Innkeeper,

Why didn't you or another innkeeper find a room for Mary and Joseph? What made you decide to let them use your stable?

Love, *(Child 3)*

(Child 3 exits, as the Innkeeper rises.)

Innkeeper: *(An older child steps forward dressed like an innkeeper and reads.)*
Dear *(Child 3),*

Bethlehem was a small village. When Caesar Augustus decreed that everyone must be registered for a taxation in the town of his ancestors, many, many people came to Bethlehem. We were not prepared to house so many travelers to our village. As it was, all the innkeepers of the city used every available space. Even the townspeople opened their homes to distant relatives, but there was not enough room.

On that night, when I looked at the couple at my door, I knew that they *must* have a place to stay. The baby was to be born soon, and so I thought of the best place I could. Our stable was attached to the inn, as they usually were, and it received warmth from the inn as well as from the animals housed there. I thought clean hay and warmth was better than no place at all. *(Pause.)* Although, if I had known who was being born, I would have given them my

Christmas Letters

own bed. The stable was not a place for the Son of God to
be born.

Signed, Innkeeper

*(The Innkeeper exits. Children come forward for the song, sung to
the tune "Venite Adoremus.")*

Song of the Innkeeper: Then on that holy night in
  Bethlehem
  No room was there to house our God made man.
  An innkeeper, in kindness, saw their plight,
  A manger was Christ's bed that blessed night.

All *(Refrain):* **Oh Jesus, Holy Babe, from Heaven above,
  You came to earth to be God's saving love.**

Congregation: "O Little Town of Bethlehem"

Letter to the Shepherd
Child 4: *(Child 4 steps forward with a letter and reads.)*
Dear Shepherd,
  What does a shepherd do? Is it lonely at night on the
hillside? On the night that Jesus was born, did you know
something was happening in Bethlehem? Were you afraid
of the angels?

Love, *(Child 4)*

(Child 4 exits, as shepherd(s) comes forward.)
Shepherd: *(An older child comes forward dressed as a shepherd
  and reads.)*
Dear *(Child 4),*
  Shepherding is an important job. When there is grass
on the hills outside the villages, shepherds take the sheep
there for food. We do not have a lot of space to grow food
for animals and so the hills help us until the weather is too
cold or wet. Then we return to the villages and use food we
have stored.
  Most shepherds like their work. At night, we sit
around and tell stories or play musical instruments and sing
songs. Often these are songs of praise to God, called Psalms.
We feel close to God when we are out in nature.

On the night that Jesus was born we were watching the sheep as usual, but that night we had noticed a special brightness in the sky over Bethlehem. We wondered what it might be. Suddenly, the Heaven seemed to open with a brilliant light, and we were very frightened. Some shepherds covered their eyes and some fell to their knees. The angel's voice filled the sky and others joined in telling us about the miracle in Bethlehem. It was then we understood about the strange light and some of us decided to go into Bethlehem and see for ourselves what the angels told us.

Signed, Shepherd

(The Shepherd(s) exits. Children come forward for the song, sung to the tune "Venite Adoremus.")

Song of the Shepherds: The shepherds watched the sky
    o'er Bethlehem;
    They saw a star aglow, and wondered then.
    The heavens soon were filled with angels bright
    Who told them of the Savior born that night.
All *(Refrain):* **Oh Jesus, Holy Babe, from Heaven above,**
    You came to earth to be God's saving love.

Letter to the Angel

Child 5: *(Child 5 steps forward with a letter and reads.)*
Dear Angel,

    What is it like to be an angel? Do you know God? What do you do in Heaven? How did you feel appearing to the shepherds?

Love, (Child 5)

(As Child 5 exits, the angel(s) rises.)

Angel: *(An older child steps forward dressed as an angel and reads.)* Dear *(Child 5)*,

    Angels are God's messengers. We appear on earth to tell people important things that God wants to announce, just as we did to the shepherds on the night Jesus was born, or like we did when we appeared to Joseph and Mary. Our news is not always good news. Sometimes we bring warnings to people; we tell them what they must do to save themselves and their homes and villages.

Yes, we know God, but so do you. The difference is, we live with God now, but you must wait until God is ready for you to come to Him. When we are not delivering messages from God, we look down from Heaven and watch over you. We are not always seen, but we are always there.

The night Jesus was born was a special night for all people, as well as for angels. We brought the world the most wonderful news, that Jesus was born in Bethlehem.

Signed, Angel

(The angel(s) exits. Children come forward for the song, sung to the tune "Venite Adoremus.")

Song of the Angels: With angels' joyful news, may hearts be stirred,
   The plan for our salvation, God's own Word.
   Then sing we now the angels' song again,
   "Glory to God on high and peace to men."
All *(Refrain):* **Oh Jesus, Holy Babe, from Heaven above, You came to earth to be God's saving love.**

Letter to the baby Jesus
Child 6: *(Child 6 steps forward with a letter and reads.)*
Dear Baby Jesus,

We know You can't talk or walk yet, but we wonder how You felt coming to earth. You are God's Son, but You were born to a young woman here on earth. We wonder how You feel knowing You are our Savior. You are sinless, but You will go through pain and sorrow and disappointment, so that *our* sins are forgiven. Here You are in a lowly stable, surrounded by hay and animals, when You should be in a cradle in a palace, because You are a king.

We thank You, Jesus, for being born, for loving us, and for giving Your life so that we may also live eternally.

Love, Child 6

(Children come forward to sing.)
CHILDREN'S SONG: "Away in a Manger"

Christmas Around the World

Introduction

The Christmas service, *Christmas Around the World*, focuses on Christmas customs found in many countries. These customs, appropriately, emphasis some aspect of the Christmas story.

The program is written as readings. One reading is from the Bible and is most appropriately read by one child. The commentaries which follow may be read by more than one child by having a different child for each paragraph. The children may read from stands or if the program is in the sanctuary the children may read from the pulpit and lectern with a riser so that the little ones may be seen and heard.

A small artificial or real Christmas tree, at least four feet in height, is placed forward on center stage. If the tree is small, it may be placed on a low table to be seen by the congregation or audience. Following the commentary readings, selected children will hang ornaments on the Christmas tree, as indicated by the script.

Music selections for this program are only suggestions. Whether the carols are sung by the congregation or only the children may be determined by the program director.

This Christmas program does not require costuming, but traditional costumes from various countries may be worn, if available, to enhance the program.

Following is a printed *Bulletin/Program Format*. The *Script* is printed separately.

Advent Activity

During Advent, the children have an opportunity to prepare for Christmas by making Christmas tree decorations which are used in the Christmas program.

The size of the tree will determine the number of ornaments needed. Extra ornaments, as well as the ones used in the program, may be given to the children following the program to take home for their own Christmas trees.

The five designs used in the children's program are: a bell, a heart, a star, an angel, and a small bunch of straw tied together with ribbon. The first four ornaments may be made of heavy paper, colored and decorated by the children to create individual ornaments. Small packages of straw may be purchased at craft stores or Christmas stores. Using clear fishing line, the bundles may be wound so that they hold together and then tied with a bow of selected Christmas ribbon and decorated with Christmas garland, if desired. The same ornament may be assigned to a class, or each student may select a design of his or her choice from the five types needed for the program.

Bulletin/Program Format

Welcome

Congregation: "O Come, All Ye Faithful"

Opening: *(All rise.)* From Numbers 24:17; John 12:46; Luke 2:17, 18; and Mark 16:15

Leader: A star will come out of Jacob; a scepter will rise out of Israel. And Jesus said, "I have come into the world as a light, so that no one who believes in me should stay in darkness."

All: Jesus, our bright morning star, you were born to bring light to a darkened world, help us to let our light shine, so that all may know you through us.

Leader: And shepherds made known what had been told them about the child and all who heard it were amazed. And Jesus said, "Go into all the world and preach the good news to all creation."

All: May we, today, feel the same joy and amazement as the shepherds, and proclaim the Good News to all people.

Leader: Let us pray. Heavenly Father, we were commanded to be your disciples, serving as an example and teaching all people about your plan for salvation. As we celebrate our Christmas here, let us remember that although Christmas is celebrated all around the world, there are still those who do not know you. Help us to be your disciples.

All: Amen.

(Please be seated.)

The Presentation:

Bible Reading 1: From Numbers 24:17, Romans 15:12, Revelation 22:16

Customs About Christmas Stars
(Children place star decorations on the Christmas tree.)
Congregation: "The First Noel"

Bible Reading 2: Luke 2: 1-7
Customs About the Animals
(Children place small bundles of straw decorations on the Christmas tree.)

Children's Carol: "O Come, Little Children"

Bible Reading 3: Luke 2:8-14
Customs About the Angels' Message of Peace
(Children place angel decorations on the Christmas tree.)

Congregation: "Hark! the Herald Angels Sing"

Bible Reading 4: Luke 2:15, 16
Customs About the Nativity
(Children place heart decorations on the Christmas tree.)

Children's Carol: "Away in a Manger"

Bible Reading 5: Luke 2:17-20
Customs About Christmas Bells
(Children place bell decorations on the Christmas tree.)

Children's Choir: "Ding, Dong Merrily on High"
The Prayer:
Leader: Dearest Lord, we thank You for this gift which we celebrate, the birth of Your Son, the Babe of Bethlehem. As we see the Christmas tree decorated with symbols of this celebration, help us to decorate our lives with the same joy and wonder as the shepherds felt on that first Christmas night. We ask You to bring peace and love and joy to all the nations, as we join the world in the celebration of Jesus' birth. And now we join in the prayer which He taught us.
All: The Lord's Prayer

Recessional Carol: "Joy to the World!"

Script

(Two or more children come forward; one to the pulpit and the others to the lectern. One child reads the Bible Reading and the others read the commentary.)

Bible Reading 1: Reading from Numbers 24:17, Romans 15:12, Revelation 22:16. "I see him, but not now; I behold him, but not near. A star will come out of Jacob; a scepter will rise out of Israel." And again, Isaiah says, "The Root of Jesse will spring up, one who will arise to rule over the nations; the Gentiles will hope in him." . . . And Jesus said, "I am the Root and the Offspring of David, and the bright Morning Star."

Customs About Christmas Stars

At Christmas we see many stars. They decorate homes and Christmas trees. The star is a symbol of Jesus, the star out of Jacob, the bright morning star. Many countries have Christmas traditions about stars.

In Poland on Christmas Eve, the children watch the sky until the first star appears. Then they call out, "I see the first star." That signals the beginning of the Festival of Stars. After the evening meal the "Star Man" who is usually the village priest visits the homes and tests the children on their catechisms. The children who answer well are given special treats of nuts and fruit.

In Alaska, boys and girls carry star figures from house to house, singing carols and hoping for treats.

In India, most people are not Christians. Those who are, like to tell the story of Jesus. In south India at Christmas, clay lamps are filled with oil and a piece of twisted cotton is used for a wick. When evening comes, these lamps are lit and placed on the edge of the low flat roofs of the houses— so each house twinkles with lights, like stars. People who pass say, "Why do you have lights on your house." Then the Christian families tell the story of Jesus' birth.

We place stars on the tree as a reminder that Jesus is our bright and morning star.

(The children exit. Selected children come forward with star decorations and place them on the small tree which is on center stage. They return to their seats during the hymn.)

CONGREGATION: "The First Noel"

(As the carol ends, two or more children come forward to the pulpit and lectern or reading stands.)

Bible Reading 2: Reading from Luke 2:1-7. In those days Caesar Augustus issued a decree that a census should be taken of the entire Roman world. (This was the first census that took place while Quirinius was governor of Syria.) And everyone went to his own town to register. So Joseph also went up from the town of Nazareth in Galilee to Judea, to Bethlehem the town of David, because he belonged to the house and line of David. He went there to register with Mary, who was pledged to be married to him and was expecting a child. While they were there, the time came for the baby to be born, and she gave birth to her firstborn, a son. She wrapped him in cloths and placed him in a manger, because there was no room for them in the inn.

Customs About the Animals

In many countries, animals are honored at Christmas for two reasons. According to tradition, animals and birds in the stable were the only witnesses to Jesus' birth, and also tradition says it was the warm breathe of the animals that helped to keep Mary and Joseph and the Baby Jesus warm.

Part of the Christmas celebration for children in Mexico is the pinata. These are animals and birds made out of paper which are filled with candy and small toys. The pinatas represent the animals and birds who were at the stable when Jesus was born. They are hung from a rope. Children are blindfolded and given a stick to try to find the pinata and break it. Then all the children hurry to pick up the treats.

In many countries, animals are given special treats on Christmas. In Germany, children carry their pets into the house on Christmas Eve to get the first view of the Christmas tree, and the animals are given extra food on Christmas, even food from the family table.

In Austria, a special Christmas tree in the town square is decorated with pieces of bread for the birds. In some areas, sheaves of grain are placed on tall poles as treats for the birds.

The animals remind us that Jesus, the Son of God, was not born in a palace or even an inn, but He was born in a humble stable and His crib was a food trough for the animals, a manger. We place bundles of straw on the tree as a reminder of Jesus' humble birth.

(Readers exit. Selected children come forward with decorations made by bundling straw into Christmas ornaments and place them on the Christmas tree. The children then return to their seats.)

CHILDREN'S CAROL: "O Come, Little Children"

(After the carol, two or more children come forward to the reading areas.)

Bible Reading 3: Reading from Luke 2:8-14. And there were shepherds living out in the fields nearby, keeping watch over their flocks at night. An angel of the Lord appeared to them, and the glory of the Lord shone around them, and they were terrified. But the angel said to them, "Do not be afraid. I bring you good news of great joy that will be for all the people. Today in the town of David a Savior has been born to you; he is Christ the Lord. This will be a sign to you: You will find a baby wrapped in cloths and lying in a manger." Suddenly a great company of the heavenly host appeared with the angel, praising God and saying, "Glory to God in the highest, and on earth peace to men on whom his favor rests."

Customs About the Angel's Message of Peace

At Christmas, we see many pictures and decorations of angels. It was the angels who brought the message of Jesus' birth to the shepherds, and it was the angels who also brought the message of peace to the whole world.

Peace and kindness have been an important part of Christmas. Sunday schools and churches collect gifts for needy families, people donate money on street corners to help buy toys and food for children and their families. People try very hard to avoid arguments and to solve problems at Christmas. Even countries at war have stopped firing their weapons on Christmas.

In Japan, Sunday school children collect money during the year and save it for their Christmas celebration. They buy flowers which they give to those who help them during the year. Often these gifts are given to people like the local police who help to keep safety and peace in the community.

In New Guinea, warring tribes would form a peace treaty by exchanging an infant son from each tribe. This child was called a *peace child*. The tribes would take very good care of their adopted sons, so they did nothing to break their peace treaty. Missionaries used this custom to explain the story of Christmas and Jesus' birth by telling them that Jesus was given to them from God as a *peace child* for all the people of the world.

Many countries have traditions that symbolize peace. In Russia and Poland, a "peace wafer", like our communion wafer, is part of the Christmas Eve dinner. And in Lebanon, part of the Christmas service is the passing of the peace. The priest begins and each person touches the person on his right repeating the words of the angels, "Glory to God in the highest and peace to his people on earth."

We place angels on the tree as a reminder of the messages that the angel's brought to earth, messages of peace and of the birth of our Savior.

(Readers exit. Children come forward with angel ornaments to

Christmas Around the World

decorate the Christmas tree. They return to their seats during the carol.)

CONGREGATION: "Hark! the Herald Angels Sing"

(As the carol ends, two or more children take their places for the readings.)

Bible Reading 4: Reading from Luke 2:15, 16. When the angels had left them and gone into heaven, the shepherds said to one another, "Let's go to Bethlehem and see this thing that has happened, which the Lord has told us about." So they hurried off and found Mary and Joseph, and the baby, who was lying in the manger.

Customs About the Nativity

When we think of Christmas, we picture the stable with Mary and Joseph and the baby Jesus in the manger. Many homes have nativity scenes that include the animals, the shepherds, and the wise men.

In Mexico the townspeople act out the scene of Mary and Joseph trying to find a place for the night. This is called a posada which means lodging. When it is evening, people from the town and many children dressed like shepherds march through the streets with live goats and sheep. Some children carry a display made from clay of Mary riding a donkey and Joseph walking in front and an angel following. They go from house to house asking for lodging until finally they come to the posada that represents the stable. The words they say are:

        Joseph: We come from Nazareth.

            We beg lodging.

            Please open. My beloved wife is weary.

        Housekeeper: Please go away, and stop bothering us.

            Or the master will come and

            Drive you away with sticks.

(Then, they come to the Inn.)

        Joseph: My beloved wife is Mary,

Queen of heaven.
She will be mother of the holy Child.
Innkeeper: Come in, holy pilgrims,
Come into our humble dwelling,
Come into our hearts.
The night is one of joy, of joy
For here beneath our roof
We shelter the mother of God.

The first manger scene was created by St. Francis of Assisi in a cave outside a small town in Italy. It was made up of live people and live animals. The only character not living was the baby Jesus which was life sized, but made from wax. On Christmas Eve, people from all around came to see the wonderful sight. St. Francis thought this made Jesus' birth seem more real to the people, and he encouraged the children to gather round the manger as they sang songs and danced with joy.

Just like those children, Christmas puts much joy in our hearts. We hang hearts on the Christmas tree as a symbol of God's great love for us when He gave us His only Son, Jesus.

(Readers exit. Other children come forward to decorate the Christmas tree with heart ornaments. They, then, join the other children for the Children's Carol.)

CHILDREN'S CAROL: "Away in a Manger"
(As children are seated, two or more children come forward for the final readings.)

Bible Reading 5: Reading from Luke 2:17-20. When they had seen him, they spread the word concerning what had been told them about this child, and all who heard it were amazed at what the shepherds said to them. But Mary treasured up all these things and pondered them in her heart. The shepherds returned, glorifying and praising God for all the things they had heard and seen, which were just as they had been told.

Customs About Christmas Bells.

The shepherds ran out among the people with excitement telling the wonderful things that they had heard and seen. Today, we as Christians share the good news with those we meet. On Christmas, though, the Christmas bells are often thought of as a way to remind all people of Jesus' birth and to ring out the wonderful news.

We know Jesus' birth is part of God's plan for our salvation and by this plan Jesus has conquered the Devil. So as we hear the bells at Christmas, we remember God's gift of eternal life to all believers through Jesus.

In parts of Africa, churches do not have bells. Instead drums are used to announce Christmas Day. Before the sun rises the first drum calls out. Adults and children run outside in the darkness, saying, "Come to Worship God, Come to Worship God." They walk to the church which is often miles away. In the church, each person brings a "Joy Gift " which is money they have saved all year as a gift of joy to the baby Jesus.

In Ghana where they do have bells, church bells ring and call the worshipers to church. The people march down the street shouting, "Egbona hee, egbona hee! Egogo Vo!" which means "Christ is coming! Christ is Coming! He is near."

We hang bells on the Christmas tree, as a symbol of our joy for the gift God has given to us, Jesus our Savior.

(The children exit. Other children come forward with bell ornaments to decorate the Christmas tree and are then seated. The children's choir comes forward to sing their anthem.)

CHILDREN'S CHOIR: "Ding, Dong Merrily on High"
(Publisher: Theodore Presser Co. Bryn Mawr, PA. "I Heard the Bells on Christmas Day" may be substituted.)
(Children are seated for final prayer before recessional.)

Christmas Around the World

BIBLIOGRAPHY

Barth, Edna. *Holly, Reindeer, Colored Lights: The Story of Christmas Symbols.* New York: Clarion Books, 1971.

Holman Bible Dictionary for Windows. Iowa: Parson's Technology, Inc., 1994.

Keller, Werner. *The Bible as History.* New York: William Morrow and Company, 1956.

Miles, Clement. *Christmas Customs and Traditions: Their History and Significance.* New York: Dover Publications, Inc., 1976.

Milne, Jean. *Fiesta Time in Latin America.* Los Angeles: The Ward Ritchie Press, 1965.

Ridley, Jackie, Editor. *Christmas Around the World: A Celebration.* Dover, Poole: New Orchard Edition, 1985.

Stein, Jess, ed. *The Random House Dictionary.* New York: Random House Inc., 1980.

Walhof, Karen, ed. *Worship Blueprints.* Minneapolis, Augsburg Publishing House, 1980.

Werenecke, Herbert H. *Celebrating Christmas Around the World.* Philadelphia: The Westminster Press, 1962.

Werenecke, Herbert H. *Christmas Customs Around the World.* Philadelphia: The Westminster Press, 1975